IN POSITION

Lauris Edmond is the author of twelve previous volumes of poetry, including *Seasons and Creatures* (Bloodaxe Books, 1992) and *New and Selected Poems* (Bloodaxe Books, 1992). Her most recent single collections were *Summer near the Arctic Circle* (Oxford University Press, 1988) and *Scenes from a Small City* (Daphne Brasell Associates, Wellington, 1994). Her latest collection is *In Position* (Bloodaxe Books, 1997). *In Middle Air* received the P.E.N. New Zealand Best First Book Award, and her *Selected Poems* won the Commonwealth Poetry Prize in 1985. She has written a number of plays for radio and one novel, *High Country Weather*. Her three volumes of autobiography were published as a single volume, *The Autobiography of Lauris Edmond*, in 1994 (Bridget Williams Books / Auckland University Press, New Zealand). She lives in Wellington, New Zealand.

IN POSITION

Lauris Edmond

BLOODAXE BOOKS

Copyright © Lauris Edmond 1997

ISBN: 1 85224 371 6

First published 1997 by
Bloodaxe Books Ltd,
P.O. Box 1SN,
Newcastle upon Tyne NE99 1SN.

Bloodaxe Books Ltd acknowledges
the financial assistance of Northern Arts.

Cover printing by J. Thomson Colour Printers Ltd, Glasgow.

Printed in Great Britain by
Cromwell Press Ltd, Broughton Gifford, Melksham, Wiltshire.

For Lindsay and Denis

Acknowledgements

Acknowledgements are due to the editors of the following publications in which some of these poems first appeared: *Into the Nineties: Post-Colonial Women's Writing* (Dangaroo Press, 1994), *Kunapipi*, *Landfall*, *The Malahat Review*, *Metro*, *NZ Books*, *NZ Listener*, *PN Review*, *Poetry Canada*, *The Poet's Voice*, *Printout*, *Salzburg* (NZ issue) and *Southerly*.

'Square-dance theme' was requested for, and read at, a multi-dimensional concert given in Wellington by the Jazz Association to commemorate the New Zealand Sesquicentennial.

'Nuclear bomb test, Mururoa Atoll, 6 September 1996' was commissioned for *Below the Surface: Words and Images in Protest at French Testing on Mururoa* (Vintage New Zealand, 1995).

'Trapeze' was commissioned by Radio New Zealand National Programme, and the section 'In Position' was broadcast on the Concert Programme of Radio New Zealand, read by Frances Edmond, with music composed by Dorothy Buchanan.

'Subliminal', 'Jonquils', 'Summer, Golden Bay', 'November', 'Letters' and 'Discovery' were published in New Zealand in *Selected Poems 1975-1994* (Bridget Williams Books, 1994).

Contents

I *In Position*

Going north

My life is a map with an arrow pointing
YOU ARE HERE – I peer at it as visitors to town
stand in the street before notice boards
...here is north, east... I see a room
stiff with foreign furniture, a street of strangers.

Now it's a hillside deep in cushions
of elephant grass overlooking grey water,
pohutukawas in fading crimson,
the sand below wreathed in its cottony tangles
balls of red hair blown here
by yesterday's wind;

for today it is mine, this great lump of land,
scratch of the grass, salt tide below;
so I sit here, wait, though there is nothing
to come. How do we live in the days that we have?

How do we learn to occupy the great rooms
of the hours that open before us
each morning? It's as though time itself
enters with the light, the first birdsong,
saying THERE – find something to cover this
empty floor, get yourself by some means across
to the other side. Will you run round

batting your head against walls,
lie down to induce patience, take a hammer
to the airy obstructions before you? Dream of
tomorrow? I spoke once to a man who said
writing poems is his delight,
also his curse; it never leaves him,
cannot make him happy. I think days themselves
are the curse, the burden you cannot put down
however it bruises your every step.

I watch where it takes me. Far down the cliff
the tide is sliding away, sinuous as fishes;
I will go down and walk on the beach.

Talking to friends

All day they walk with me about my
fretful rooms; at last the air no longer
charges round the house nor slaps against
the walls, as in my roaring yesterdays.

Glasses of wine take on in their hands
a healing property – carrot juice for
the soul perhaps, with cinnamon. Lunch
inscrutably becomes medicinal. They

cannot stop the rain weeping at my windows,
yet this afternoon I saw how mist on
the harbour had become a Whistler's Thames
and little Wellington, a London.

I like the way they shift their chairs,
their bodies exchanging piquant messages
then turn to me, alert and purposeful, graduates
from a private refresher course in love.

In position

I want to tell you about time, how strangely
it behaves when you haven't got much of it left:
after 60 say, or 70, when you'd think it would

find itself squeezed so hard that like melting
ice it would surely begin to shrink, each day
looking smaller and smaller – well, it's not so.

The rules change, a single hour can grow huge
and quiet, full of reflections like an old river,
its slow-turning eddies and whirls showing you

every face of your life in a fluid design –
your children for instance, how you see them
deepened and changed, not merely by age, but by

time itself, its wide and luminous eye; and you
realise at last that your every gift to them – love,
your very life, should they need it – will not

and cannot come back; it wasn't a gift at all
but a borrowing, a baton for them to pass on in
their turn. Look, there they are in this

shimmering distance, rushing through their kind
of time, moving faster than you yet not catching up.
You're alone. And slowly you begin to discern

the queer outline of what's to come: the bend in
the river beyond which, moving steadily, head up
(you hope), you will simply vanish from sight.

Flying is a violent act

Ladies and gentlemen the time in Baltimore is 8.41 a.m.
If you wish to adjust your watches 8.41 is correct
and this is Baltimore.

The plane snores steadily on
but the docile machine at my wrist
repeats its last instruction:

2.15 on a cloudy afternoon in Earls Court Road, London
slightly south. It is as though it alone remembered to carry
the paraphernalia of departure – that prudent
polishing off of the last overripe nectarines,
my rage at the orange cat's nervous defection ('must be shut
out when you go'), outside

the young man, black, dishevelled-drunk, lurching about
among pots of white petunias that smelled of
fresh rain on dry leaves; then
the self-condemning labour of luggage…

There it ends. The afternoon, the night to follow –
did I leave them behind, throw them out? Did they put up
any sort of fight to continue? It seems not; it was
instinctive resignation.
I moved out casually beyond darkness and the clock.

I forgot about days, their precious opportunities,
their spaciousness, their small surprises. Such treasure
there was, and I (with British Caledonian Airways)
tossed it away without a moment's thought. A day deserves
better; the reverence we accord to hallowed things:

A day is all we have, it is a newborn child,
a miracle, pure blessing, the undeserved unlooked-for
compensation
for all the foolish
squandering of ourselves we did the day before.

Hanging my head I wind my watch and drink
the death, the indestructibility of days
in thin airline champagne.

Body language

I have a black blood blister under
the nail, third finger, left hand. Slowly,
slowly, it grows towards its end, with

the little protein pack wherein
it lodges – fleck of inconsequence
I notice as I wait with others to board

the big jet. We shiver beneath our
lassitude at this supervised wrench
from the sustaining ground, yet I find

a nervous glee in taking my single self,
my truth and nothing but...beyond
the common bounds. I can shed my teasing

accumulations, duties to friends, put down
those small shaky saucers of concern I offer
to my children, theirs; turn off the silent

cacophony of shock, exasperation, urgency and
love that scrapes its strings above a thousand
conversations. I am apart now, a single sack

of hopeful grains, organic maps like fingernails
and hair; unwatched in another country, yet
quite coherently, I'll grow – or practise

the ageing body's programmed perseverence: I
think when I return my blemish will be more than
half way up the nail. So the geography of

every journey's printed here, so growth prepares
its own defeat, visible logic to remind me
every death or ending is a consummation.

Autumn in Canada

Naturally, it's the fall – what else could it be,
this loosening, letting go, these faint purposeful
dry showers, the crushed mosaic under my feet?
The fall. It passes through me with an airy rustle

as though I too relinquish a burden – and I look back
to its first season, to the young.woman who looks
now so angular, so unpruned, sweating her way through
nights of longing, mornings bereft and absurd;

tears, and the long explanations to follow – all that
buffeting, the unmerciful spring weather of the heart.
How fiercely each cell and sinew had then to hold
together! Beside me on the grass walk hundreds of

big dark birds: 'Canada geese,' says an old woman
on a bench, 'they come every year.' Sea birds awkward
on land, carrying within their oddly asymmetrical bodies
a map of the seasons they too know by the signs.

Taking down Christmas decorations

I was first in this room twenty years ago;
alone I crouched on a bare floor, leaned
on the low window sill, and looked I think for a sign:
was this the place which might take us
quietly through the difficult days, and at the end
put each one carefully, steadfastly to rest;

where the death which had made vagrants of us
in our own house, and now followed us everywhere,
might sit down and speak at last with
a low-toned, trusting sorrow.

The October sun lay coolly across the floor,
but outside a high wind rocked the sea, battered
the harsh and tangled hillside plants:
and I made some kind of wordless affirmation
of earth and water and weather,
and the unremitting struggle of growth.

This Christmas children were here, perched on
the furniture, tacking up cardboard stars and trees,
reaching up to tie shiny things
to the tree's bristled branches, its piney smell
fresh and sharp. This morning as I drag it over the floor
the smell still hangs within its spiky niches.

Always after celebration there are small griefs,
a coming down, the old apprehensions still
waiting about unchanged. Yet I am glad to be here.
We have neither solved nor relieved our loss;
rather it has come with us,
we live in its constant knowledge. Each
Christmas is now, or the last she spent
with us, or the one to come.

And hills are instructive: whatever grows
here, every green cell, pinprick of sap, knows
in its very fibre that to live
and breathe at all is to act provisionally –

as yesterday's imperial pohutukawa blooms
lie today in piles of reddish furze; it's there
from a ledge I throw the faded little pine.

Lake Tutira

Late afternoon. Two black swans
glide to the edge on flawless glass.
There they pause, erect, austere
in their Modigliani slenderness,

then slowly turn their crimson bills,
the feathered oval of their heads –
above, below in perfect replica,
as though to say we honest swans

have come to prove we know and speak
the entire, unarguable truth. Each
quiver, every queenly curve appears
within, without, the same: appearance

and reality harmonised at last.
The silent crystal of the lake exists
for this. The smaller ovals of their
eyes do not, and will not, blink.

Hymn to the body

You see them in tea shops and drapery departments,
old women holding carefully to their intimate,
patient, unspoken knowledge of an approaching decay.

They are encased in chiffon, full-sleeved
blouses, high necks, soft-falling skirts, brooches –
considerate fictions prefiguring a later disguise,

one they have seen with the nightmare eye that
occasionally opens within them, contemplates the horror
of foreign stuff (chemically treated cotton wool,

perhaps silicone, they imagine) which briefly will
serve as flesh when flesh itself has made its last
retreat. They shake themselves, return to shopping

or chat. Yet they know too, as I do, that living
and dying spring from the same root, and there is
still the shuttered bedroom, dark mirror in which

the impaired body may yet see itself quiver with
that frisking of nerves that points the heart's
direction, stirs an old, unthinking delight.

Ah the wise body, so to declare itself for love,
and the inextinguishable hope of love, so to stand up
and shout its sweet defiance into the silence.

The heat of summer

It's barely light, and out in the tree tops
cicadas already are shrieking high noon –

how absolutely, with what high assurance,
the sharp little creatures live at the heart

of their days, wearing the weather, the daylight
and dark, right up close to the skin; as though

to be alive at all – to wake up – is to act, and
to shout of it. I'm put to shame, leaning drably

here at the door, not dressed, hoping somehow
to avoid struggling into the morning, clumsy

and ill-fitting as I know mine will be. Soon
others will wake, we'll remember yesterday's

quarrels, this innocent jubilation will dry up
like dew. And truly, cicadas themselves must

some time face predators, hunger, high winds;
they grow old and die. Well, what if they do –

it's now, they're out doing their marvellous
rhythmic hysteria, and I hear them. Hallelujah.

Locations

In a rainy spring my house is often dark:
I stare from the kitchen window at grey and silver
weather drifting past; close to the misted glass
a box of scarlet impatiens flowers holds out

minute green saucers to the rain, and to me in
my solitude, my beautiful imprisonment, inscribed
as it is with living green, with wild or sensuous
skies. Down in the bus shelter, at Courtenay Place

the old man will be staring outwards too, his
ancient tweed unkempt, his beard a yellow rag;
he'll watch the rain, its gentle repetitious
wetting of his entrances and exits – he who has

so many, and so few. His eyes are watery,
blue-white, half closed in muted calculation:
he too pursues his appetites – a roof, a drink,
a word – his passage over gritty asphalt

in the shelterless rain and frost, his only
gardens City Council plots. He is the stranger
who watches with me in a grieving privacy,
the friend to whom I shall never speak a word.

Take one

Tonight I walked on the wood-smelling verandah,
in the treetops the starlings were slowing
their shrillness to an inconsequential whisper,

the geraniums giving out their sweet herbal smell
even after sundown in the late summer air;
boatmen were beetling over the bay, centipedes

out on some energetic inscrutable mission – and
I thought, this is my time: I don't have it
for long, and the way here was never easy:

sorrow sat often like a beggar under a bridge
darkening its passages and corners, and some days
it moves so fast I am too tired to catch it –

but whatever it does, while I'm here nobody else
can have it. They wouldn't feel its kick, or
understand this gleam in its eyes, and I do.

II *Subliminal*

Subliminal

So like him, and so cruelly unlike, this
pale thing dressed up in the grey suit,
white shirt, dark tie he always chose for
funerals – presumptuous facsimile, no more;
I hate its spurious command, its way of
claiming, hour by wordless hour, to be

the version authorised, the only one extant.
How could my friend agree to such diminishment?
A sort of rage possesses me – yet as the silence
perseveres, its very changelessness begins a change
in me I look again, and see the aching shadow
of his age, the walking stick he didn't like,

the paling eyes; and further back, the younger,
sharper man he used to be. It's living itself
that weakens all our faculties; how little
in the end could he remember even what they were,
the sunlit future promises of long ago. I want
to say 'Hard going, then?' and take his hand.

But suddenly, as though he's heard and answered
me, I know there's something else, a pleasure
– yes, almost – in finding at last you do not have
to take another single breath. Now I can
touch his cold unnatural skin quite easily.
It's not so very different from my own.

A family event

There was a chair by the bed – no, not a bed,
though he slept in it past all exhaustion
and in his own room. We brought friends,

one who stood at his feet and addressed him
formally: *teacher, rangatira*; 'I take something
of him wherever I go,' he said at the door.

Children ran past, chasing and laughing, and
'Tea, more tea – ' called a voice from the kitchen.
I went back to him then and stood at the window

looking out at his garden, neutral already, and
still. Two-year-old Grace ran in and climbed up
on the chair; 'Oo!' she squealed, touching

his hand, 'isn't he cold!' and gave him a daisy.
So, variously, we took our instruation, strange
runes without a code. The first day his chest

still moved with the breath we couldn't imagine
gone; but the unchanging days taught us well, and
at the end we were ready. They came to take him

to church, we gathered round, each kissed that
pale stone effigy, understanding at last that
our love had left him, and he didn't care.

The wife

Your name, your name! Here, in the paper:
I stare at it stupidly, attached as it is
to these brief unmanageable facts – was born,

is dead. They say it's you, gone like this
without a word into an impenetrable privacy.
A new, cold ignorance begins to spread across

the foolish years where I, hoarding it
like old brass, duller every time I looked,
kept some small persistent hope of happiness.

It's said they are most homesick who leave
home in pain or rage – is this the reason
for my stiff repudiation, outrage even, that

so lacks the healing purity of grief? Come
back I cry, come back and tell me that our
better selves aren't lost irretrievably.

The husband

Listen, the night was cold, I woke up restless,
headachy, dissatisfied with everything; the bed,
the room, the chilly dark, its distance from
the morning – ah but morning too. If you like,
my life. Like an untidy cupboard it was full
of things I didn't want, and searching through

the muddle never seemed to turn up what I did.
My head got worse, a light somewhere went on
and off, and then – you mustn't mind – there was
this marvellous sheet of flame that swept across
and took it all; me too. I didn't even think
of you; the kids a bit, but after all they left

us long ago. Yes, I know what you will say –
the memories, we two as we were, glowing in a
greengage world... sorry, can't help you with that
either. You see, the condition of my condition is
I don't – remember. The flame took that as well.
Even you can't change this. There now, let it go.

Local knowledge

Main Street, Tuesday. Shoppers meandering,
doors wide to the mild October afternoon;

the little town restored to itself, that just
a week ago was given to its sorrow, every

lesser occupation put aside. Death in
the village; everyone assured, in place,

the vicar's being to explain the words, the songs
to the family arriving from their other towns.

Strange reversal, that in such tribal protocol
we should find ourselves the guests. So it was

that late in the day we left him, covered over
in their windswept village graveyard,

knowing finally that we had long ago
relinquished him to those who with no thought

of definition had taken him for brother,
father, son. With them he was at home.

The pace of change

'Not unconscious, no. The patient's
brain died hours ago.' But look – your skin
is warm to touch; lying back, eyes closed,
you labour fiercely. Something in you
cries out still for struggle, effort:
this is how it is to be alive, to fight
moment by moment to achieve each
rasping, shuddering sob of breath.

I lean down, labouring too, as if by
endlessly repeating names of things
we know I can reverse the tide of blood
they say has taken you. Nothing changes.
Stupidly I try again. Then see at last
the body's terrible sorrow. Poor breath,
that cannot speak a word: how shrewd,
how manifold were once its languages.

One to one

Love ends, as it began, in a flash.
Lightning splits the heart, breaks root
and trunk at a stroke and scatters
debris everywhere. Driving across

a bridge on a winter day, the water
dark below, I came to this sheer end.
No warning. Two unfleshed tendrils
in the brain leapt their tragic gap.

However I protested later I was fond
of you, insisted we must keep in touch...
I knew that nothing could again
connect what that day put asunder.

It's all one now. Your answer's
here: this pale immobile face,
the marbled hands, the odour of
embalming. The truth we now would

both agree is instantaneous, and
cannot be revoked. My loss I thought
struck then, midway across the bridge,
all later compromise the merest fiddle.

Your death is my correction.
It is as though you said why then
hold on to anything – the loss
of love is all, and lasts for ever.

Good behaviour

The time has gone for lies
and the kindness of lies –
the quick falsity 'How glad –'
'Yes, do –' 'Love from –'
the whole flimsy language of
intention. The ugly truth
of this old marble thing,
face-and-body-shaped, now
is all we know, and mean.

Games played with the living
sound in this commanding silence
trivial, or quaint, or cruel;
yet since I now lack means
for all eternity to make him
laugh, look up, briefly forget
the pain of living that so fell
upon him, day by day – well,
I'm glad I told him lies.

Marriage

Marriage, that old silly thing, that play
so long rehearsed, so indifferently performed,
so slow in later scenes to recreate the liquid
flightline of that gentle, passionate pas de deux

we knew as novices. Now I'm to think of it as
something closed – dénouement, final lines: except
for this, your going home without me. Home? Some
evil epilogue it is, that I should stand alone

here in the wind, you in the ground, alone too
with the dull pulse of stones, earth's clogging
dialogue. Did I then not think that we would end
at all? I cannot tell. Thinking was mere distraction

once, the trick being, lock our breath together,
fall together, and the spinning hot river would
carry us away; the children always, like a prompt,
alert at breakfast time. Let me not think of it

nor speak. Let the silence come and stand
beside me so I know it is the end. You're gone;
as for the crowd, the populous years, the friends
who so delighted us, all that went long ago.

Spring afternoon, Dunedin

We lay in the long grass on the hill
high up near the crooked quince tree
and out of sight of the house.
The afternoon touched us with its
fragile sun – and then the mountain
suddenly reached up and took it.
So *early* – it was barely three
o'clock. Together we looked up

from our books and shivered,
then pulled up the rug and
hand in hand, talking of altitudes
and moons, we wandered home. Just so,
in a grass-sweet patch on a little
planet were we spinning minute by
minute out of our brightness and
into the changed, unloving years.

III *The Itch of Permanence*

A literary age

I am not mad like Yeats's Crazy Jane
nor half asleep, nor touched by spells,

nor given to raging at the lost hours
of a regretted, virtuous youth. Ulysses

suits me better, the journey beyond journeys,
unimaginable frontiers, some risky

passionate vista: *the baths of all
the western stars* quiver above my sleep.

The nervous public speaker

She wore a red jacket –
it lit up the distance
with the dark gleam
Black Doris plums have
before they ripen,
or a crimson hibiscus.

Among suited shoulders
earth-black, she grew
like a flower, a flame,
cell of light in the careful
dimness audiences create.
Perched on my risky rock

I kept looking up, watching
for that bright centre –
the door that opens to
a first chink of morning
in a windowless hut,
the safety of sun.

Falter or freeze as I might,
this shimmer of love
remained; my daughter,
with me this side of the dark;
nest of joy perched
on a trembling branch.

Trapeze

She is a flare of crimson light in the dark
a nerve of motion
arms open she flies alone
a crucifixion of longing.

Our hands are wet with fear.

In her lyric expectation
she soars to the narrow bar:
released one second after its time
it comes down twisting,
not straight,
held as though by the hesitations
of an uncertain lover.

And so she falls.

no cramp of the wings
no clotting of that fluid body
no sound but the gasp we do not know we give.

The sun and moon have fallen into the earth
gravity has swallowed the air. My eyes
are dry and fiercely hot, staring
into that burning streak.

There's the net. There's a moving tangle,
a roll, a rolling, something that begins to rise
and stand   and stretch
and valiantly at last to wave.

But we stay slumped in the high ringed seats
some spirit in us
that never left earth before
has gone too far. We are weak with loss.
We can do nothing. We watch and wait.

And now it happens; she dazzles again
but it is our hands that reach and touch
and find the place. Our breath.
We hold the strong bar.

So she has taken us; she has drawn us
into herself for ever.

Matauri Bay

Two women, a dog, a boy crunching the pebbles,
shining curve of water; islands, fine clouds
of sandflies and seagulls against the sun:

to travel my own country is to come upon scenes
so familiar they glow with the eloquent sheen
of old possessions, yet I never was here before.

What is it then, this possession? Do I cover the sea
and sky with my homely treasures, scorching afternoons
on the beach, dinghy rides out to another island?

The day stares me out. This water broke without
ceasing across the glinting sand, far before
the Rainbow Warrior had its sea burial here,

before the flag pole, the famous equivocal signing,
before the oldest canoes nosed around the headland.
All footprints are the same beneath the tide.

A matter of timing

A line of daffodils growing along a fence
bright gold, upright and sure, the clouds above
blowing about like washing; and the first willows
coming into leaf, a pale and tentative web.

They are perfect, it all is. And I know every detail
by heart – five-wire fence, a post every few feet,
staples old but tidily hammered in, small flat lawn,
path to the gate. An absolute dream, total as

childhood. The shock is, it isn't mine. It must
have slipped out one day, been found and taken in
by a neighbour. I glare at her, plump woman standing
in the doorway to watch me driving slowly by.

Undeserved

The smell of rain
has in it an old sweet solace;
night, and the scorching day
lying like dust in every crevice of air –

and then this sudden benediction:
perhaps we couldn't help it,
that mean act,
our dryness of spirit,

the torpor we dragged about all day –
now, after all, we are to be forgiven;
that oddly herbal emanation
rises from the earth like incense.

Bronze in a town square,
city of Derry, Northern Ireland

I walked round them, touched their
black-green surfaces, arms, hands, even (shyly)
a cheek. He was going 'out there'; colonies
gleamed in his narrowed eyes. He strained forward,
his son too, altogether convinced, grinning,
scarcely able to wait to begin.

But the women, wife, girl, looked back.
The folds of their skirts were skewed, uneven
at the hem; and I thought how Rodin had shaped
the bare body of his terrible Balzac
again and again, till its anguish would show through
the heaps of clothes he knew the stone must wear.

The women would go; nothing else for it,
but you could see they would always carry within them
the first shock, the inexplicable silence between letters,
the 'never again' as they woke early
to the bright, empty morning waiting outside
to be laboriously imagined, always beginning from nothing.

Love story

This thing you call love – what is it then?
An insect that buzzes and frets in the night,

a breathing monster with hippopotamus feet that
glares above you before it tramples you down

some say it's a rose – and do they include
the aphids that swarm on its slender stalk?

I knew a capacious mansion where footsteps
crowded the shining floor; but the light died

and I was alone in a tunnel of sorrow that led
from the door; love then was a whip, a furnace,

a falling from cliffs shaken by earthquake to
the bloodstained rocks below. Yet here, this

morning, is this beautiful child, with love
as a cluster of birds singing unrepentant

about his head, each note a scratch on the air
that he feels like a feather in his heart,

delicious and tickling: so he laughs and runs,
stopping only to explain that today, a world first,

he found out how to hop. And he does. Twice. Really
it's hopeless, love. It hasn't learnt a thing.

Tree surgeon

To plant a tree, to bend and heave and sweat
contending with the hillside's stubborn clay,
to settle about the slim young wood
its prepared place – and to do this at a death –
is to set a naked tendril beside the abyss.

And yet we do it – I did. This was her tree.
And indeed these great leafy arms for twenty years
tossed the weather about the sky, and in their
creak and rustle lived the chanting of her name.
Her brief abandonment, her eager authority,

her sorrow; her body dancing in the autumn wind.
She died young. *So far, so fast*, the tree man says
this morning, looking down from his platform
in the fork, as though he knew he spoke of her;
slowly takes up his saw, then stops again.

They're beautiful, these silver dollar gums,
but their life is short. Of course you knew this
when you planted here, so close beside the house –
I turn away. To know? What is this knowing?
I was merely there when life and growth began.

The arrival

Death is a city more remote than all my arduous
imaginings. I saw only the leaving for it –

no, not even that; the place of leaving.
I hurried, frantic while there still was time,

but time itself had shut like a flower, a day lily,
folded quickly after sundown, and she with it,

leaving face and hair that were mere substance,
things of shape and colour; nothing. I turned away.

I had missed her then. She had already made
a home in the unimaginable town, the room

beyond rooms, place without place, cold where
coldness has no temperature. What business

had I with this stony replica? 'Barely an hour,'
they said. An hour? A million years – it does not

signify. I can make up time and distance as I
choose. She has left them, and she does not care.

The mirror

I cross, recross the room, his little
heavy body close against my shoulder,
willing him back to sleep, then turn and

there we are, dim but accurate, as though
the glass itself created us. I with
the beseeching shadow in the eyes, holding

him, wet eyelashes curved across his untried
perfect cheek, so he'll believe the treacherous
world is safe for him; and all the years

between us whirling about, birds flying in
from the broad wheatfields of time
while we two pause a moment at the edge –

tiny Austin, feet not yet for walking, I far on
along my many roads. And then I take him
to his cot and stand watching, while he sleeps

his way into his life. He is my guest,
my gift, the royal offering that is always
to be given away to someone else.

Out to lunch

So I say to my serious brother
You're a handyman, you know how to fix
things, a tap, a plug, some flappy thing
you can see needs a staple in the right corner

Oh yeah he says frowning (*is this conversation?*)
and I tell him of this kid who thinks
fixing things is something you buy, so he
shrugs, gives his back-to-front grin

Crikey what a mess if you didn't just do it
and much later after more wine
and the tarte de citron and two espressos,
when I start on cultural inheritance, family traditions,

all that – he's my grandson, this boy –
he says Well I dunno, he can come to the lab
if he likes, see what I do with my photos.
So I kiss him, my dumb fix-it brilliant brother.

Pilgrimage

The high old house is here, and lived in too,
the same gallimaufry of porches, gables,
stained glass windows in the panelled doors,
verandahs broad as church hall floors;

and the pebbly river down the back, still sidling
about its rocks and shallows out of the bush
and into the flickering sun – it's a tapestry
of dense familiarity, yet everything I came to find

is gone. Those crazy, passionate, fateful years
have left no single echo, not a whisper. I am
a stranger, standing about alone, unrecognised.
Perhaps even ghosts tire at last, they have their time

amd when it ends, they roll up like a dusty mat
the living residue they were left to hold, and vanish
into a larger, older time where none can tell who
speaks, or when or why, or even what they mean.

Jonquils

(for Kathy)

I remember the cold slide of my hands
on the stalks down, down to the locked knot
where each green column began;

and the wrenching, the slithering grip
till it bent over, slipped, came
at last (perhaps pulling up buried inches

from deep in the ground); then the adding
of huge handfuls to the heap at the edge,
while a strong sweetness flooded

our faces, sap dropped its cold syrup
on our feet and the wind swirled in the trees.
It was August, the spring of every year

of our lives was there on that slippery
bank as we gathered the white armfuls,
shouting in the wind and laughing,

taking with us the whole sappy morning,
a delicate load, to put in glass jars
on tables in kitchens all across the world.

Summer, Golden Bay

A strong current rises, charging
through my surprised body and on
to the head, where I begin as usual
to talk of it. Scholars once said
the humours were in the belly, or lower:
so they are. This crunch of cold sand
under my bare feet is a source, an essence;
absolute. Do my feet laugh, exaggerate,

bury themselves in these coarse grains,
this rough invasion, bright gold as it is?
Of course. So harsh a kiss is to be
received, returned, like any other.

Body's the cathedral; to think of it
is merely to go singing in its choir.

November

1 *Morning*

Yes. Yes, it is. The first hint of
a musical whisper – it's miraculous, absurd:

the moon's still up, and that can't be
light, that grey sketch of a shadow

of leaves against what I suppose is
the sky. At the door the air holds out

a cool hand. Shall I go out? I could,
I'm alone – I could step out of everything,

even my skin, speak to the world in
private, alone. Maybe never come back.

The birds are so tender, so good, they don't
have a reason, it's a blink of daylight

in their eyes, that's all. Imagine that
being enough to make you want to sing.

2 *Evening*

These long white evenings induce
a kind of waiting; on the verandah
the windless air itself stands still,

the sun, the gold of day, long gone
yet darkness not arrived – just this
pause, a straight questioning: the day,

the year. In early summer the year closes
as schools do, composing their reports.
Two friends lost – not to death but to anger,

that illness of the spirit. I stare over
the sea, greying now with dusk; this is
an indifferent account to hold out for

assessment. Loss ages us more harshly than
the mere passing of time. The air, cooling
quickly, has grown thin. It hurts to breathe.

Letters

I met her only once, this quiet wife
who cooked his dinners, slept beside him
forty years and now has brought them to
an ending with, it seems, her usual carefulness,

simply by not waking up one morning. Earlier
today I took his letter down to the harbour,
sat on the pitted concrete wall among
the silent boys with fishing rods; a flock

of yachts stood up before us, white, becalmed
upon the steely water. Look, I said to my grieving
friend, how they preserve an air of stately
purpose despite the lack of wind; but of course

he turned away. Home now among the debris of
my screwed-up letters I know that I must
go to him. Only the body's helpless silences
can speak a language he will understand.

Interlude in Zambia

He smiles and smiles – indeed we both persist
in radiance. 'How kind –' I begin, 'your house –'
and wish he'd turn the colour TV down. I sweat
among the protruding vinyl chairs. It's a relief

to go outside and walk through head-high
grasses, cross to the shady pens his families
of creatures occupy. So, this is subsistence
farming...The mammoth trees, their flowers like

violent birds, save us from the sun as we meander
past his geese and piglets, little lordly goats,
cows with their great gloaming faces up against
the bars; then there's the maize, a fish pond,

the huge grasses never far away – and all the time
we two, reaching for conversation: he thinks he'll marry
a second wife. Oh. Will the present one object? No
place for that, George knows 'normal' when he sees it.

What if she in turn should want another man? For
a moment he dislikes me, glares at such unpleasant
lack of tact. Yet afterwards his black hand takes
a good strong hold of mine, poor parchment thing

we both perceive it is. 'I liked the little pigs,'
I say, and shuffle off towards the jungly grass.
'The cobras,' calls my host '– you must take care.
They do not like at all to be surprised.'

Train journey

The green countryside
the amethyst hills; the sea.
The world. I learnt its molecular structure

once, glimpsed the delicate dance
of DNA through the lens of a childish formula.
Now it's my failing subject –

the window of my train shows me dirty England
growing plastic bags and Coke tins
on its unkempt river banks;

acid showers from Europe
wither the ancient trees. Unloved land where love
is the body's healthy cell: poor earth,

neglected child and flouted parent
in the wretched kitchen of history. Suddenly
through the rattle of rails I think of Max

at home – ten thousand miles away – his small new feet
holding the floor, the ground, seizing potency
with every step, factory poisons further off

for him than wars or rumours; he laughs
and stumbles, grabs the marvellous mother air
he can't imagine will not always love him back.

Nuclear bomb test, Mururoa Atoll, 6 September 1995

I am water   I am sand
I am a cell in the trembling earth
I am a shaken pebble on the hurt sea floor

a young fish made ill by the predator poison
coursing towards me across the ocean
that was my friend;

I am the child's brown toes
curling back from the tumult of gravel
at tide's edge grown suddenly dangerous and sharp

I am the hand, the foot, the easily bleeding veins
the skin that a monstrous tearing apart
of the air may lift from the flesh;

I am the woman beaten to blindness by a flash in the sky
the orphan staggering about my dark; I am
the fear of every creature for grotesque adventures

of brilliant men. Call to me in my fear,
cry for me, take me from the tainted earth
that was my home, the ground where in an instant

the innermost cell of life may have no place,
tell me what I must do when the simplest act of living
is undone and turned to chaos.

The contest

Brixton station. Umbrellas at every angle.
The turbulent, good-tempered crowd.
Our unwitting agreement
to shove, be shoved; in some weird
way we're a team

and the captain
exhorts us – yes indeed, we see
we must do better. JESUS! he yells
(how inconsequential our heaving
and grunting) JESUS – march for Him!

MARCH! By a passionate choreography
he's a machine, a hurdy-gurdy, a whole circus
black limbs spinning in the gleam
of the rain. You march for jobs
he roars, houses, money – all nothing –

JESUS IS ALL   He is love!
He is tall!
He is everything!

Now we can't look
We're dropping the ball
we're going to lose

but thank God he's hero material
he keeps smiling JESUS we hear JESUS
as shamefully, faster and faster
we scuttle round corners
pushing our feeble anonymous selves off home.

Discovery

Midnight in the breathing dark,
I walk through the house,
lit from beyond itself by the light

of the city, translucence of
moonlight, white stars asleep
on the harbour water. This is

home, I whisper, amazed. If
anything is mine it is this
luminous gift held out across

the unknowing dark. Last week
I was busy in airports, pursuing
the traveller's ridiculous industry

of survival, each moment bursting
with trifles like over-stuffed
luggage. In this stillness I neither

lift nor handle, I stand at the window,
weighing nothing, carrying nothing.
I breathe, and the light grows

within me. Home is where your life
holds you in its hand and, when
it is ready, puts you quietly down.

Square-dance theme

I

You, Clara Eliza, five-foot legendary grandmother,
battling wood fires in a freezing dawn,

riding to town with an empty purse, the old man
blank with booze – I can see you, moving about

in the dim grey weather where history lodges;
it whirls like fog over the Poukawa farm; now

it clears, and you're there in the gig, reining in
a bolting horse, three terrified children

gripping your skirt... – I think I have always
known you, from tales that had their first telling

three years before I was born, when consumption
at last devoured you. August little lady, you used

every second of your dense half century creating
a clan, taking for materials your doggedness,

imagination, love. It's time, you know, that we met
more exactly – if a generation's twenty years,

three lie already between us. I step forward,
take your small calloused hand: the skin's weathered,

quite dark, but your brown eyes are sharp and –
no one had told me this – glinting with laughter.

II

Now I turn to the clearer quotidian weather
of morning and evening; no ambiguous mist here

but streets, houses, a room festooned with
the treasures of 13-year-old occupation –

RUTH up in extravagant colours, photos, plants,
books, and you at the centre, dark-eyed girl,

first grandchild, with the velvet bloom skin
and already humorous smile. Let me tell you

of long-dead Clara, show you the silent peak
of the mind on which I stand, looking back

a whole century to her, forward to you,
sweetly alive here, carrying like a lively germ

the secrets of future time – including, I believe,
outrageous machines humming away in houses

of magic where you will easily come and go. But
to family matters: that small long-skirted woman

used all her wisdom, her staunchness, to nourish
her children. You too, daughter of many daughters,

latest inheritor, will likely give birth to a girl
who in turn will depart for a later, stranger time.

III

We pick up and carry this baggage, each for a spell
conceiving our labour as mothers with passion,

and a fine and healing delight; we grow
larger of heart as we learn to allow our pain.

And each of us plucks from the present, as
a new fruit, a variant, is added to earlier strains.

I cannot know yours, though I guess that
the brilliant brushwork in this open scrap-book

will one day declare you the artist, the woman.
Grandmamma Clara wrenched from her back-country farm

skill with horses, and with medecines found
in the bush; but you will mature among women

with a larger pride in their powers. Take what
we offer, the learnt habits, the faith; respect them,

and alter them. Hers was a raw land, yours knows
itself older and darker; like us you will make

new garments of old and durable threads. Take my hand
now, as I took and held hers, feel the current,

the tingle of courage she passes through me to you.
Keep it and use it, through unimaginable beginnings.